TWO TONGUES

CLAUDINE TOUTOUNGI grew up in Warwickshire and studied English and French at Trinity College, Oxford University. After a Master's at Goldsmiths, she trained as an actor at LAMDA and worked as a BBC Radio Drama producer and English teacher. As a dramatist, her plays *Bit Part* and *Slipping* have been produced by The Stephen Joseph Theatre. She adapted *Slipping* for BBC Radio 4, after it featured in a reading series at New York's Lark Play Development Centre. Other work for BBC Radio includes *Deliverers*, *Home Front*, *The Inheritors* and *Based on a True Story*. She lives in Cambridge.

Also by Claudine Toutoungi, from Carcanet

Smoothie

TWO TONGUES

Claudine Toutoungi

CARCANET

First published in Great Britain in 2020 by
Carcanet
Alliance House, 30 Cross Street
Manchester M2 7AQ
www.carcanet.co.uk

A CIP catalogue record for this book is
available from the British Library.

ISBN 978 1 80017 000 1

Book design by Andrew Latimer
Printed in Great Britain by SRP Ltd, Exeter, Devon

The publisher acknowledges financial
assistance from Arts Council England.

CONTENTS

TWO TONGUES

RIFT

Pretend it's August. Pretend there's sunlight on bare arms, dappled
water, louche, marauding ducks.

Pretend the sheep wear serious faces, slouch in groins of gouged-out
rocks and far-off human chatter's growing slack,

losing all heft until there's nothing on the breeze but buzzards
mewling. Nothing more incomprehensible than that,

nothing more consoling.

CHRONIC WAITING ZONE

These are the daylight hours but
we absorb beneath the surface

tepid lighting, shrink (*Feet
please!*) for a husband-wheeling

woman, fixate on trollied
notes and staff who pass

and pass... Does anyone believe
in all this striding? Or the litany of

strange stranger names: *Shahido
Hulk? Dawn Carrier? Angela*

Chart? Something is up.
Something is very definitely

crawly and dark on the outskirts
of our vision. A girl tells Hazel

on reception they were 9.15 and
now it's 12.08. Gets back *We go*

by numbers here, not times
and X and V and Y start

crawling and if it's just a
black dot on the horizon why's it

following us? What do
we do if it ripens?

It's hot. Not letting up.
We could strip.

Quiet today says Hazel.
I like it.

DOMESTIC FOX PHYSIOGNOMY

The conclusion reached by Russian scientists after decades
spent domesticating foxes was profound but hardly unexpected:
if you're going to be tame, be cute. Less chance you'll be flushed

down the toilet. I think about that on brutal baby-filled
commutes and whether any of the team, Goran say, or Vlad,
ever mistook a certain cub's white markings for a bib and

placed it in a bassinet – fell to coddling it with sugar cubes, toy
ducks and songs about the wide embracing arms of Mother
Russia. Gave it earmuffs. Made it a scarf.

BY SMALL SIGNS WE BETRAY OURSELVES

People know when you are not quite right.

Even if you're merely one who'd like to wear a fez
and stroll about, requesting *mumkin titkallam shway shway?*

because you like your fez
(you had it from your grandfather)

and because you'd like them to talk slowly, please,
you've sunk four hundred on Beginners Arabic

 – people know.

Even the light caught between the blinds casts
a jaundiced eye on your aspersions.

What you want is not what you think you want.

You think you want tousled hair and kissed shoulders.
You think you want beetroot and ham hock and to rub

your head against his shin
like a cat but what it amounts to is

 – people know.

They know you put your faith in soda powder
swallowed by the vat to neutralise your internal acidity.

Muffled as you are with sluicing,
mottled as you are with mossy teeth,

miniature as you are,
you can't keep hiding.

The amygdala knows its own agenda.
The hippocampus, lately, likes to grass.

ACUITY INDEX I

I know a dishcloth from a satin kimono.
I know a beagador from a butternut squash.
I know a scythe from a semi-automatic.
I know a moose from a rifle range.
I know a Fabergé from a dustbuster.
I know a Letitia from a cos lettuce.
I know a smurf from a small, mean intruder.
I know a smurf from a small, mean intruder.

ZUGZWANG

I am unhappy about your description of my life as dull.
It is dull but I dislike you using the word dull.

If I could I would unhook the receiver from the wall and
place it on your dirty mouth. I don't feel able to elucidate.

If you hadn't known the German for lose/lose, if you
hadn't the face of Dürer as Christ in *Self-Portrait of*

Dürer as Christ, this could have been a whole lot
easier. As it is, the slum donkeys of Marrakesh

surround me. They bray with hindsight. Their arpeggios are
pertinent – this is not a metaphor, this is the Blue Phase which

stems from the Beige Phase. Which stems from taking too
much of a run-up, too much virtue signalling and fog, heavy

duty fog, and if, as forecasts indicate, there is to be more
fog, Lord give me the strength to be dinky and circumspect.

2 AM

Sometimes a cat in the night like a baby.
What to do with those inchoate moans?
Something that never learned how is trying
to reach you. The earth stirring. Stones.

NEW MODERN DRAMA

There are people on stages everywhere going mad in hotel
rooms shouting *fuck* and *what is it you want from me?*

This one entails a young mosquito-hating escort self-harming
with his lover's stiletto. Who do you relate to more: the escort

or the stiletto? Who do you incline to as the electronic long-
drawn whine in surround-sound with added reverb drags you

up and from your seat into the scene? Watch: now I am hitting
myself around the face because I believe I have contracted

dengue fever. Now I am sloshing ice cubes from the minibar into my
pants to cool my genitals. Now I am betraying you on my pretend

hands-free with my pretend younger lover who is also betraying me
with my mother. Now I am prone on the coverlet, now I am writhing

under strobe lights. Now the strobe is out, the set wrecked, I am here, hyper-
ventilating I am still here goddamn it what is it you want from me what is it?

DISCLAIMER

Lapsang souchong is the colour picked for our apartment walls and the
internet does not tempt me. Landslide in South East Province kills teen
backpackers and the internet does not tempt me. Have a soggy sense
of politics, intend to oven-crisp it and the internet does not tempt me.
Likes Viszlas, keeps Coonhounds, stir-fries Tufted Vetch and the
internet does not tempt me. Car-bombed vivisectionist you dated found
AIDS cure in monkeys and the internet does not tempt me. The old kinds
of boiler wear out, smart ones wear fume hoods, kvetch in forums about
storm damage; how I got over it, how I suffered rust, how I knew it was
an Act of God and the internet on no account tempts me.

NOT MY BEST WORK

I am endeavouring to write
not my best work.

The onus – how I love the word
onus – is all on me.

It is a cup I cannot
not sup from.

It is a hurdle I cannot
vault o'er.

I should go to a hilltop alone and hunker down in a cave and
        then come back
down and write it.

But I am afraid of bats.

It is a life goal.

It is a long road with very infrequent waterholes.

I am not man enough.

I am insufficiently
male but I can and I must

begin.

THE AGE OF INVENTION

all this kowtowing to nature
gets right up my antihistamine-addicted nose

some days for lunch I have cheese
on cheese with additional cheese on top

it's all I can do to shave
and then sit around clean-shaven like a bad

backfired joke with no pun
line I mean punchline whatever who cares

it was never going to work I knew
it the minute I read the cheese label

up close and saw it wasn't
cheese it was some shit called aioli

dip who needs that not me not anyone
I call my Mum and say Mum

they have a machine now
a robot that can do the lawn

yes she says I know
I am the robot

HUNGARIANS

There are a lot of Hungarians
around at the moment.
Hungarians in the park.
Hungarians in Tesco's.
Hogy vagy? they say.
Hogy vagy? I say,
though it's my only words.
That man in the street
making a racket,
he's Hungarian and the one
who trundles past each day at four
with the trolley and the crocodile
hat, a hat for hunting crocodiles
I mean – don't be fooled.
He's not Australian.
He might want to be Australian but
he's Hungarian. All of them are.
Even the one called Lee-Jeong
Zhang and Neil Webb, he's Hungarian.
Oh very Hungarian. When you come
down to it every single
one of them's Hungarian.
Even you.

ACUITY INDEX II

Taking into account my *muy bien* inability to judge distances and my *muy bien* hangdog look on most weekdays in the first and second quarters not to mention my apparent lack of cheer in the third and final quarters, my approach is changing with stealth and a new kind of optimism known as brandy. Or *muy bien* brandy. In this way without recourse to hair shirts or hot coals I urge myself onwards through inclement weather and *muy bien* sea-mists and send out from the other side of hope dispatches resembling abstract arrangements of Kalamata olives in side-garnishes laden with *muy bien* symbolism. I keep a wary eye out for subtext in all the wrong places, internalised vacuity, disparagement, pseudo-disparagement, hate crimes, self-hate crimes and war, the net result of which is war.

STUMPERY

It shouldn't be possible
should it

in a shut-in maze of
flagrantly arthritic

witches' fingers to
drift and feel so vaporous

knots harpoons fuck
-you Vs not you not

here surely
with so much hard

knock stuff to snag on
bark turning its snarling

back tangled
imprecations and nothing

underfoot but mosses

breathing *come down*
here dear
thing

down to join the riven and the cauterized

PLEA

There should be more poems
    about the Biblioburro of La Gloria

they bray in five or so tongues
   cite Stevenson and Spinoza

this pair, known fondly
    as Beto and Alfa

like Moore's *the cure for loneliness*
   is solitude and chunks of apocrypha

hee-hawed in bursts as the rays batter down
     (as the rays tend to do in Colombia)

panniers of books banging flanks and the flies –
      don't even start on the flies

CHIAROSCURO

Feeling of late even more
deracinated than usual

and finding a quartz, tinkly rosary in her father's old cigar box

she began to talk
privately in public places

parks, station platforms, open places, conscious with every
stone of how

she let herself be picked
up and put down often

and wishing for firmer categories

aware of being
neither the little angel

clinging to the off-white ankle of Christ

nor the shadowy Magdalene
slipping away

and not unhappy about this

(though some days to be
either blind or definitely a seer would be simpler)

she kept on

fumbling
towards salvation

as if you could muster it

as if you could force a miracle
out of the rushing air.

SEQUOIA

Such haughty candour you say
as we wander past the giant redwood
in the botanical woodland.

Or it might have been *grandeur.*
Hard to tell when the wind is
permanently off the leash and everything's
kinetic – our brains, our hair.

Or maybe it was *canyons.*
Such haughty canyons
you might have said, trailing off
to remember some past hinterland
out west. Red rocks. Dusty slopes. A bare
forked tree, acrimonious
against the incandescent sky.

Then again... canyons... redwoods...
do they go together?

This one, this elder, if it knows
doesn't give the answer.

It has set its roots down
amidst larkspur and monkshood
and made its peace with English
rain and feral winds and its own
many, gathering
convolutions.

GLACIAL ERRATICS

we drank unpasteurised milk in the valley

we imbibed the non-compliant polyamorous air in the valley

we got in touch with our authentic rage in the valley

we made inroads into inroads in the valley

we took the tops of our heads off in the valley

we held as 'twere a mirror up to nature in the valley

we ate the flesh of the valley

we bathed in glacial flour in the valley

we got a sort of stupid crush on the valley

we objectified the valley

we to some extent coerced the valley

and to a lesser extent empowered the valley

we bought shares in the valley

we lost everything at the casino in the valley

we exhausted the valley

we denuded the valley

we discussed whether it was *hedg-emony* or *hegg-emony* in the valley

we put ourselves through eccentric contractions in the valley

we died intestate in the valley

we came back to life in the valley

we expected a hell of a lot from the valley

we forgot the names of what we were looking at in the valley

we glowered in the valley

we wore approach shoes in the valley

we diagnosed a handful of complaints in the valley

we had a case of the vapours in the valley

we melted, thaw'd and resolv'd into a dew in the valley

we were entirely transparent in the valley

we added our innate natural charm to the innate natural charm of the
valley

THE LAST KITTIWAKE

is not performing
will not adopt a grandiloquent tone

or rouse up a skirling
lament on camaraderie

loss and the dip
in sand eels

hootless

non-wheedling

the last kittiwake has
no comment

regards the bay
from a sea-smashed cliff face

forgets what it used to find
uproarious

i.m. John Lanchbery

CUSP

I am taking up a new position
spreadeagled on the shingle

welded by the half-baked
sun to the earth's crust, a

washed-up starfish
draggled with bladderwrack

(several suppurating encrustations
microscopically concealed) and

watched over by a smoked fish
shack and scrupulously attentive

monolithic ear in the shape of
Scallop, steely listening Scallop

shoring up the hiss of distant
breakers, drifters, deep six

defiers, revenants. Salt
-wrecked but not drowned.

SHIPWRECK

Leitmotifs of gorgeous hempen verisimilitude cower in the corners
of the frigate where the obstreperous raven insists upon itself. Gloom-
mongers cheer but others of us are far more interested in the scaly
bone-crunching worms causing surface tension and the small molecules
of green. I know I should do something with the torso and the teeth but
wherefore and to what end? How to triangulate the coordinates in some
meaningful equation that eases both soul and synovial fluid and does not
dismay the lank polypi about the rafters nor agitate the herculean molluscs
festooning the poop. Sideswipes won't be tolerated nor lichen permitted
to rot the public weal in clumps. The Sleeper, be assured, sleeps.

MODERN SONG

You on Edward Said on Theodore
Adorno on Beethoven
aloud

is hot.

It is. Fundamentally. Go on. You
are. Say it again.

Say it in triplicate

– the part about his Late
Style or Spätstil.

Spätstil. Spätstil

you make me want to run about in muddy fields and riff off
blackcaps and ruin dank shoes you make me want to tamper

with closure and bring down bourgeois structure and spend
every single one of my   remaining days   rapt

in the pursuit of an

                  abstruse

                            motif

some

       dense

              disintegrating

          appoggiatura

emptying itself outward

                – like forever

CONTORTIONIST

in the blackest recesses of Bistro Malatesta entre les heures du quatre
   à cinq
(forgoing his liaison with Odette for the third time in as many days)
   Prudhomme observes a snailfish

undulating round the hat stand's spine, the stalagmites of candles (its
   sad, small eyes, its cryptic lack of scales)

wants to cleave to it

wants to shake the dipsomaniac in the corner, hiss *Ay caramba! Have
   you seen it? Here on the Rue Mouffetard – so far from deep-sea
   canyons, so far from home?*

considers eating it flavoured with rosemary, flavoured with dill

whiskery thing

sees it, loses it in Gauloise furls, catches it again, its curl/uncurl
   progression along a velveteen banquette

it stirs him – its decision in oblivion to be a thing of light and so
   gelatinous

thinks of turtles nibbled at by surgeonfish

wonders if perhaps he's lost his grip, and if he has,
likes it

THERE ARE MUSHROOMS IN THE GALLERY

enoki   reishi

formal and informal modes aside, the curator would like it to be known
    that

there are mushrooms in the gallery

lion's mane   oyster

and whilst the artist's project may be to provoke reflection upon
    impermanence and friability

the curator would urge you to remember that

there are mushrooms in the gallery

and the gallery cannot be held accountable for those who undergo

paroxysms   seizures   respiratory arrests

even though it's true they have put mushrooms in the gallery

also expressions of racist and homophobic views which the curator is at
    pains to point out
do not reflect the ethos of the gallery

but mostly there are mushrooms in the gallery

shaggy inkcap   astringent panus

not in clay or giclée but real

actual mushrooms in the gallery

and if you are uplifted, if you are edified, as the artist may
intend, by the codification of mushroom as

symbol of tufts and spring

small male homunculus bowed as if in penance

clairvoyant   knight errant   usurper   sage

mushroom as icon of resistance

mushroom as emblem of a pluralistic utopia

blight-blaster   wayfarer

portal 'twixt heaven and earth

the curator will concur

– yes it is uplifting

be uplifted

but stay alert

because there are mushrooms in the gallery

SEVERAL MISOGYNISTIC REMARKS BEFORE BREAKFAST

to which I could do wizened and perplexed
                              as good as any maestro.

I could do the tetchiness of Chekhov
                              on the afternoon his samovar ran dry

and what irked him most wasn't thirst
                              but the parching recognition he was widely

misunderstood and that no one
                              not his public, not directors, not his wife

grasped the full twistiness of his opus.
                              I could. I can.

But *A woman's brain lacks the plasticity of a man's.*
                              I put my head in my hands

like Henrik Ibsen at the Grand Café in Edvard Munch's
                              Henrik Ibsen at the Grand Café.

SUSPENSION

after Anthony Gormley's Edge III *sculpture*

nothing so much in this bare room
as a body involved

in a procedure of lying
heels perpendicular to the wall

three feet above the ground
not a body easy

to be reckoned with
blistering skin

nothing resembling
eyes only kilo

on kilo
of cast-iron mass

face up
if you can call it a face

contemplating
what?

not rust not leverage not what it means to topple or
be toppled

it both speculates and
floats some way beyond

hairless
very pleasing calves

it might say identity
is fiction

if its mouth
were more than the suggestion of a mouth

but its axioms its quips
its saws hang

ceremoniously mute
several metres up

unpinioned
plinth-free

WHY I AM IN LOVE WITH YOU

As Chief Inspector Dreyfus of the Sûreté
your sangfroid sagged in stages.

Your wits, clinging to the Eastern cliffs of your mind,
relaxed their fingers.

Satan's imps
tugged at the strings of your lips.

Beneath your eye, that muscle
quivered like a flea.

O Lom! O Herbert!
The perfection of your mouldings!

I see you now fumble with your cigar-cutter,
chop off the tip of your little finger. Laugh.

THE MARMOTS ARE SUFFOCATING

J'admire votre hérisson
you tell the woman in the artisanal cake shop
because it isn't every day you see a chocolate-sculpted
hedgehog

and in the forest glade
upon discovering that all wild bees
are welcome at the bee hotel you ask the hive
and what about les abeilles domestiques?

the hive makes no reply

likewise the mountains
– textbook blanket
silence

and
you
below
overcompensating

filling the void with topic after random chitchat topic: *le kilomètre
vertical,* the recipe for *tartiflette,* the conjunction of the sirocco
and foehn that blew a little bird straight through the restaurant,
the cat Macaroon *(perdu ou volé)* and the writing on the wall in
the tunnel under the bridge (*ici les marmottes suffoquent*)

HUNTER FORAGER

in the night I rose up and ate sweet peppers, celery and a plump vine-ripe
    tomato far more tomato-like than its insipid sibling consumed earlier
    that day
I was distracted by another resignation
one more in a line of abdications at a time when... *clear-thinking... strategic*
    deals... impossible to brook further delay...
I drifted and my nose I admit was out of joint
something infernal and malign in an email from before – condescension
    masquerading as tact and a panel had come down in the yard and
    there were
things in the bed... magnifiers... microphones... strictly speaking nothing was
    as it should be
dictation from an unknown source
running in my ear through a comprehensive list of my infractions with
    additional reflections on the imminent collapse of all things versus the
    elasticity of the soul
hard to tell at 3.12 if the soul would win
at 3.14 I rose again and swept my floor like an old-time Palaeolithic Wife
I was content and no birds sang except one bird whose call was a regular
truffly snore which gave me comfort until I joined him

WELSH RETREAT

There is the Chuckling Bird and the Typewriter Bird and in the toilet there is
a Manx Shearwater, wheezing. No one has told it there will be vegan
ginger cake at four. No one has spoken of the druids to it or instructed it in
quilt-making or helped unleash its shakti through a course in slow-flow yoga.

It has not practised PIGEON SPREADS ITS WINGS or FISHERMAN CASTS
ITS NET in a tai chi one-to-one tailored to its particular needs. *Bore da, Bore
da* we say stepping closer to the water closet it has mistaken for its burrow.
Our cells vibrate in sympathy. We can accommodate it. We are enlightened.

BYGONES

Take some love letters sent way back,
way back when people wrote letters and loved you,
loved you like a slobbering dog,
a slobbering, barrelling dog you couldn't dodge.
I couldn't dodge it. That was your apology to Annie when she met you in
 the café,
finally, in Café Bernhardt with its four tables,
four tiny tables and twenty-four eyes
and her eyes. Licks of gas ready to go off.
Did she have to go and lob that coffee at you?
Coffee sloshing everywhere – in your hair, your ear ducts, down your top,
your itty-bitty snowflakes top,
snowflakes Aiden kissed you in.
Aiden kissed first you said. *And you kissed back.* That was all you got
 from her:
instead of reparation, a baptism.
A hot coffee baptism. Then the stares.

CUMBERBATCH

I was talking to Benedict last night
on the steps of the old church hall.
We were wearing our socks and
holding our shoes in the dream
and Benedict roamed over far-flung
terrain: chronic celebrity, the quest
for authenticity, a particular energy
drink you can no longer buy. It was
springtime and nice to be shooting
the breeze with such ease and
suavity. He was soon to be filming
a movie with a mutual friend. His
role, the Martian, hers, the Amazon
Queen. It cheered my heart immensely
to picture those two on set keeping
each other company; he perhaps
suited in something prosthetic and
rubbery. She no doubt bearing a
quiver of arrows, tipped with steel,
Sun Tzu's *Art of War* on hand
from the old days.

THE THERAPISTS OF MY FRIENDS

talk to me by stealth:

in the small print of tapas menus
through gravelly Johnny Cash on a loop in a lift
via contrails, peepholes
misdirected medical reminders addressed to Mr Caro
sotto voce, over tannoys
via wind-chimes, with graffiti
in the runic configurations of ducks on a pond
in the dialect of Orvieto
in the waggle dance of bees, in
the hieroglyphs of breakfast crumbs
the amputated torsos of discarded shopfront dummies
via parking fines, in neon
in the semaphore of bedsheets on a line
contrapuntally, through static
in the hand gestures of school refusers and
in the single bark every fifth hour
of an unseen dog

TRANSLATED IN CUMBRIA

Tonight the role of the beck will be played by Tomas Tranströmer.
He will convey its swagger and rush in Swedish so punchy to those

who can speak it, so deft, the force will be almost upsetting.
For the rest there will be no translation. It will feel like

being in a fight. You won't understand but might suffer minor
cuts and abrasions. Tranströmer may even opt for Performative Dance

to express the beck's lunatic flourishes, its lachrymose leanings.
If he does, please spur him on with appreciative noises and murmurings.

The part where the beck bounds up from its ditch will touch you the most.
How it leads you by the hand in a nimble gavotte right up to the summit

of Lingmoor Fell, where the flock sit like mystics and the air is cool and you
drink up the moon from Highwaymanbeck's blaggardly slate-struck eyes.

Next time, we had hoped Robert Frost might give us his *Dry Stone Wall* but
        he turned
down all offers, citing typecasting fears and a tickly, unshiftable cough.

AMENDMENT

We would like to apologise to readers for the mistake
in last week's issue and the misspelling of the name

Claudine Toutoungi. In particular we would like to
make it clear that the person in question's surname is

not to be construed as Tutu Genie. Toutoulingi. Two
Tongue-y. Toutanjajee. Tao-Tao-Ngee. Tootle-Ingee.

Tangerini. Tchoo-Tchoo-cherini. Tallahassee.
Takahashi. Tooboogiewoogie. Tzaziki. Trincomalee.

Two-G-G. Toroo-Taralee. Tootsie. Turtle. Tut.
And furthermore she's not as foreign as she sounds.

LOST Ü

in Iskenderun or Cairo or God only knows
it fell from my name

got trampled in dirt, wasn't
scorpion-crunched but scrambled and scuttled and fashioned

from dust a magnificent hopalong gung-ho
hop and went

up
up

up to a perch in the cleft of a spindly
twig

not a halo as such nor legible
signage – construed as a fly or an optical

blur, dashed-off-forever-unfinished notation
inscrutable

scrap – a blink or a blip, caress, kiss, wince or
half of an upturned

discarded moustache
who knows?

but up there for years

nonchalant
unattributable

an *ahem,* an unnoticed
notice-me-please

elliptical

in the olive trees

THE MAN WHO LEARNED ENGLISH
FROM POETRY

on a train in a storm did not remark

Nice weather for ducks or *Looks*
grim out but once
declared

We are feeding the swans of tomorrow
yesterday's bread

and small talk desisted.
Deep time stretched out like the title of a book:
The Long Twelfth-Century View of the Anglo-Saxon Past.

APOLOGY, FOR AYANO

I am sorry I did not come through on the English conversation
after our first and only lesson. Winter here is hard, the cold
interminable and I could not take the long walk across town into
sleet to reach your house. I admit I did not uphold my end of the
bargain. I should have nailed my colours to the mast where
you and where your baby Shunto could have seen them.
Ayano, I assure you – not all the people of this land are shilly
-shalliers, fobber-offers, shifty loons, curmudgeons, dolts,
prevaricators, poltroons, lugworms, shoddy planners, hags,
hogs, sots and shameful dilly-dalliers. Not all of us. Though
in the wintertime, I grant you, it may feel like more than some.

BOGUS YOU

yes you –
where do you get off
with your brogue and
your tribalism and your
vowels, your sing-song
vowels, going on and on
about that ancient
parish vault in Monaghan
(*Oh Monaghan? Yes
Monaghan! Oh we love
Monaghan!*) and how you
found a parchment there
detailing your long line
of folk, your fake folk;
no, you did not once cop
off with Roddy Doyle's
accountant beside a
Sligo racecourse and
no, your mother's
maiden name is not
O'Shaughnessy and no,
your second cousin
never sold pills to Colm
Toíbín. No, you never
ate chips with Sharon
Horgan, you flimflam,
and even if you had
it doesn't count.

THERE SHOULD BE A NAME FOR

repeatedly banging your head against the low-hanging beam
in your holiday flat. Yes I know – classic First World. Classic
not exactly a real problem. Not like constructive dismissal

or abusive texting or rats. You take your cracked and fissured
scalp and lie on the top bunk beneath an open skylight and
let the birds of the valley sing to you in their French.

Un petit peu de pain et pas de fromage sings one. Another makes
noises from the repertoire *Sounds of Frankie Howerd.*
Ah me your sorrows shall be transmogrified by sparrows.

Little scrappy Alpine sparrows and Alpine choughs and Alpine
swifts and the addition of the prefix Alpine, guaranteed to add
mystique to even the most mundane trouble: *Alpine
dry mouth, Alpine short fuse, Alpine intermittent gloom.*

AN ENDURANCE ATHLETE HALLUCINATES HIS ABDUCTION BY ALIENS DURING THE HAWAIIAN IRONMAN TRIATHLON

It felt fine. They had me on a drip.
They extracted spinal fluid, a portion of lung.
They recorded the beats of my heart,
played them back to me on an ambient loop.
It felt fine. They had me on a drip.

Their craft was a cold space.
The uproar in my ears receded.
I was stripped back to something purer.
They inserted a nose mesh to screen out bugs.
Their craft was a cold space.

I was with them only ninety minutes.
They had seventeen words for *race*.
They purged me. This dark stuff is not
an isotonic liquid. It is my urine.
Afterwards, I looked for them in the lava fields.
I was with them only ninety minutes.

REMEMBER THE AFTERNOON WE STARED AT NOT VITAL'S *CAMEL PELVIS* IN BRUSHED STEEL?

Camels are sources of food, transport, currency
this from a booming man with beard and broad-brimmed hat he was always on
  our periphery
intoning details iterated elsewhere as if fresh prophesy
mid-June, lapwings in attendance, lashings in fact of Nature: pink ballerina
  waxcaps, sheep droppings, clouds
we squinted at them through a space in the roof of a former deer shelter
clouds and clouds and clouds and clouds and clouds until one budged an inch,
  an inch merely
but God it felt tremendous to know something was up there, moving
or maybe the deer relieved to crawl in somewhere out of the storm had left
  behind trace elements of ecstasy
or maybe it was the man who hadn't been portentous but sounded so leaving a
  void
into which had rushed joy

THE ARCHITECTURE OF SKY

doesn't tremble at solitude
isn't dwarfed by loss

the architecture of sky

isn't porticoes and palisades
pavement and brick

the architecture of sky

is the song of a robin
whose Cubist grammar

is holding us up

i.m. Emmanuel Toutoungi

INTERIOR WITH STILL LIFE

I left my eye on top of the sideboard.
It had no complaints. It wanted a
breather. It wanted to flip out, flop
free, cut loose from the grip of my
co-dependent lashes, my socket's
strictures and crap about keeping
up appearances. *Screw all that,* it
breathed, basking on tissue paper.
If it were a dog it might have rolled
over, but it didn't bother. Blissed
out in that posture. Disposed to not
take in what was on offer: wonky
mirror, ceiling crack, portion of a picnic
by Cézanne.

AFFIRMATIONS

The Plogoff Prize for Most Convincing Badinage With Plants
The Laurenson Award for Extreme Yawning
The Mitzy Duval Prize for Mild Dismay
The Bogeland McKenzie Endowment for Equanimity With Cats
The Leaf Fitzroy Prize for Low-Level Mania
The Merc Dupont Award for Brouhaha
The Wendy Sturgeon Prize for Most Persistent Rash
The Joan Husky Fellowship for Elbows
and The Malone Mayhew Endowment for Prolific Lapses in Concentra

tion

COLLABORATION

the ocean is all very well
we walked up out of it with gills I know

I know but things react badly when damp or clogged up
bread for one becomes

pasty flour soup and words
look at these fine words I wrote in the sand

indecipherable
already nibbled by eddy on eddy of salt water stuff

what outpourings
what ego – so

ok ok
you're unfathomably potent

with depths unsounded
get over it

or go on your way
grande dame in your glittering kaftan

do you think I can work with this –
your desolate sweeping gesture endlessly stealing the scene?

SELF-PORTRAIT AS A MAJOR MOTION PICTURE

I have been cast in the role of klutzy bumbler aka goofball temptress aka
    slapdash titsy-totsy rom-com heroine

it's exhausting
all this dashing along platforms

missing trains in which the beloved
is just departing

and hilariously snogging the wrong one because even my eyesight
is klutzy and the club dim

all the high-octane angst and
sensitive monologuing

and colliding with
lamp posts while ogling superfit bin men

and pouring drinks down my top out of sheer class-A
sexual tension

all that marrying a loser
spawning a child who acts as my surrogate spouse through its formative
    years
and requires therapy and develops a fetish for bacon and pills (till I ask
    myself *Is it my fault? Should I not have called him Porky as a boy?*)

and after a time becoming a compulsive wild swimmer
suffering shark bites and hallucinations

but knowing this is where I belong
this is where I find my elemental home

up against stingers
the fluorescence of predators and my own damn fool self

in deep water taming the waves with my half-crooned adorably off-key
    renditions
of Dylan of Joni of Cohen

NUMBERS

After your biggest mail-out yet to 4796 of your
closest friends and acquaintances, three replied.

One said *yes I can come.* Another said *yes I
might come.* A third said *no, I can't come.*

Then it was time for sleep because it was
Thursday and for anti-ageing purposes

you always tried to be asleep by five.
In your dream there were eight Toyotas

six Kias and a Lamborghini. You totalled
all of them in fifteen separate crashes.

Ended up in hospital where you met
a shepherd, a vegan and a gerontologist.

The shepherd taught you to count sheep
in Cumbrian – *Yan. Tyan. Tethera. Methera.*

The vegan was mute and the gerontologist
advised you to ditch the number 3, the letter

C and all your relations. *What all of them?*
you queried. *But I have 417 and that's only*

my nuclear family. In the dream it came out
as *enucleate family*, which over time got

interpreted by five psychiatrists as passive
aggression, toxic narcissism, Capgras

Syndrome, low blood pressure and angst.
You went with angst because you enjoyed

saying *Ich habe angst* and because it had the
fewest letters and because partially it was true.

LAMMAS LAND

The cows were in the margins today.
I was treading through piles of their powder-dry
elegant rejections. They were staying nice and cool in the shade
  while I was kicking up spray-storms of fallout.

A throaty warbler. A percussive cheep. Something sonic in the
  hedgerow. That was the gist of it.

You could call this an attempt at prayer. An attempt to call
  upon my higher power though someone somewhere
  would no doubt get all up in my face about it, would get
  all exercised at my choice of doxology.

O cows, how do you do this thing you do? This lingering-on-
  the-edges, this solid disregard for anything but grass?
  And air. Sometimes flies. This absence.

I have seen you running through a field fleet like horses but
  that was years ago. Clearly you don't make it a habit.

Cows, I bow to you. I will bow my head and learn.

ACUITY INDEX III

for as long as I care to remember

I have been sat on the edge of this chair

facing   facing up to   facing off with an oblong

array of yellow-lit signs   shimmering   arches and

flares   and   crooked   telegraph wires

walking the plank of an H   to waylay a

V   arm-wrestling a K   slamming into

an L and landing   slap in the lap of a fat black

Cyclops O   with whom I switch eyes for a time   to

squint   at   a   far-off   flickering

me   camping it up with the pinhole/pince-nez

suspicious art sleuth unpicking a forgery   redoubtable

dowager wielding lorgnette   cat-burglar bandit

Venetian assassin   monocular   fop

dazzled   but not   thrown off

THERE IS NO NARRATIVE

you could tell that would explain this

the marine biologist   would rush his findings to the lab

the archaeologist   would trace the hairline fracture in the
fifth-century vase with a languid murmur

the veterinarian   would lock his ketamine in the safe and
go out to walk in the long grass and
crouch beside a turbid brook to scoop up
tadpoles in the way he did as a child

LAMBS

Haven't seen a solid swan like that in
aeons and that pale lemony light sprawled
on cobbles, it's obscene, isn't it? Trust Spring
to turn up late to the party, sneezing, handing out
tracts, wanting to warm up conversations warped
by a paucity of affection. No one was fooled.
March had seen the olive trees catch blight and oceans
away a land was burning. Even the lakes were burning.
But Spring kept banging on about the lambs. It was
boring. Until days later in a field, a random sodden
field, you saw them catapulting back and forth, slinkies
gone mad, limbs and squeals and sheer unmitigated
zinginess. It stang your eyes. Made your eyes go cross-eyed
with hope, with hurt, with hope, trying to keep track of every one.